BEETLES

ASHLEY GISH

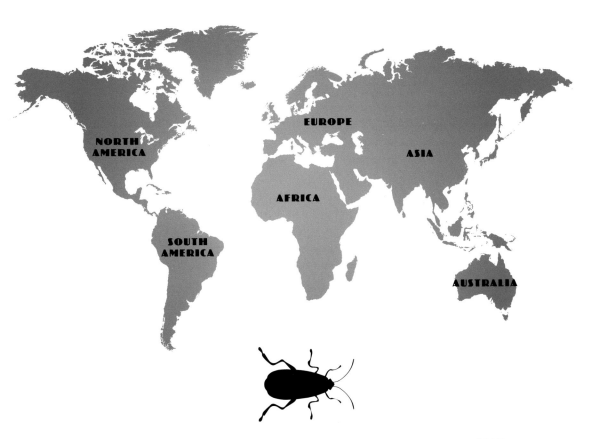

NORTH AMERICA

EUROPE

ASIA

AFRICA

SOUTH AMERICA

AUSTRALIA

CREATIVE EDUCATION · CREATIVE PAPERBACKS

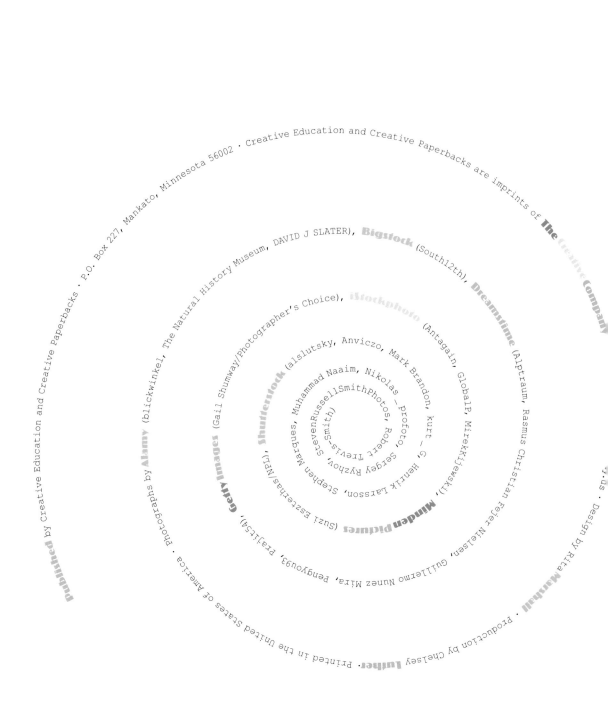

Published by Creative Education and Creative Paperbacks · P.O. Box 227, Mankato, Minnesota 56002 · Creative Education and Creative Paperbacks are imprints of The Creative Company www.thecreativecompany.us · Design by Rita Marshall · Production by Chelsey Luther · Printed in the United States of America · Photographs by Alamy (blickwinkel, The Natural History Museum, DAVID J SLATER), Bigstock (South12th), Dreamstime (Alptraum, Rasmus Christian Fejer Nielsen, Guillermo Nunez Mira, Pengyou93, Prajit1354), Getty Images (Gail Shumway/Photographer's Choice), iStockphoto (Antagain, GlobalP, Mirekkijewski), Minden Pictures (Suzi Eszterhas/NPL), Shutterstock (alslutsky, Anviczo, Mark Brandon, kurt_G, Henrik Larsson, profoto, Sergey Ryzhov, StevenRussellSmithPhotos, Robert Trevis-Smith), Stephen Marques, Muhammad Naaim, Nikolas

· Library of Congress Cataloging-in-Publication Data · Names: Gish, Ashley, author. · Title: Beetles / Ashley Gish. · Series: X-Books: Insects. · Includes index. Summary: A countdown of five of the most fascinating beetles provides thrills as readers learn about the biological, social, and hunting characteristics of these solitary, widespread insects. · Identifiers: LCCN 2017060036 / ISBN 978-1-60818-988-5 (hardcover) / ISBN 978-1-62832-615-4 (pbk) / ISBN 978-1-64000-089-6 (eBook) · Subjects: LCSH: Beetles—Juvenile literature. · Classification: LCC QL576.2 .G57 2018 / DDC 595.76—dc23
CCSS: RI.3.1-8; RI.4.1-5, 7; RI.5.1-3, 8; RI.6.1-2, 4, 7; RH.6-8.3-8
First Edition HC 9 8 7 6 5 4 3 2 1 · First Edition PBK 9 8 7 6 5 4 3 2 1

BEETLES

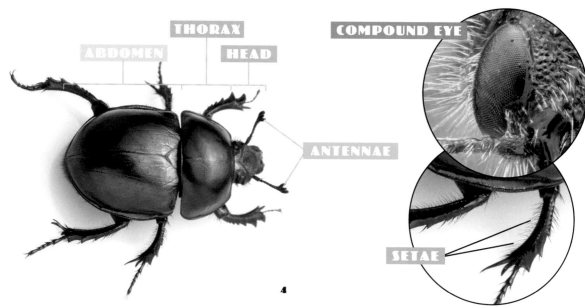

ABDOMEN

THORAX

HEAD

COMPOUND EYE

ANTENNAE

SETAE

4

XCEPTIONAL INSECTS

Beetles have hard bodies. They have strong mouthparts. Some have horns. Others can light up. Some are too small to see. Others are bigger than a human hand!

Beetle Basics

Beetles are insects. An insect's body is made up of three parts. These are the head, thorax, and abdomen. Insects also have six legs. Beetles' bodies are covered with tiny hairs called setae. The hairs are sensitive to touch, sound, smell, taste, and light.

Some beetles' heads have extreme features. Feather horned beetles have feather-like **antennae**. Most beetles have **compound eyes**. They can see many different colors. They can even see lights and colors that human eyes cannot see!

BEETLES OF THE WORLD

There are more than 350,000 kinds of beetles.
They are found on nearly every continent.

DARKLING BEETLE

DEVIL'S COACH-HORSE BEETLE

LONGHORN BEETLE

GOLIATH BEETLE

TITAN BEETLE

SAFFRON BEETLE

SMALLEST BEETLE

The smallest beetle in the world is

1/100 of an inch (0.25 mm) long.

That is the size of a grain of salt!

3.8 BYA   **PRECAMBRIAN EON**

540 MYA   **PHANEROZO**

UNITED STATES

More than 20,000 kinds of beetles exist in the United States.

OLDEST BEETLE

The oldest beetle fossil was discovered in Illinois. It is more than 300 million years old.

300 MYA

245 MYA

65 MYA

present day

ON

Adult beetles have a case around their wings. These wing cases are called elytra (el-EYE-trah). Some beetles cannot fly.

WATER STORAGE

During dry seasons, beetles can store water under their wings.

Beetles' skeletons are on the outside of their bodies. These exoskeletons vary in color. Golden tortoise beetles change from reddish-brown to shiny gold. Glorious beetles are bright green. Dogbane leaf beetles are a shiny green-orange.

Beetles use their mouthparts, or mandibles, to eat. The mandibles are strong. Some beetles are carnivores. They eat other insects, worms, or snails. Other beetles are scavengers. They eat dead animals, rotten plants, and animal **dung**. Most beetles are herbivores. They chew through plants.

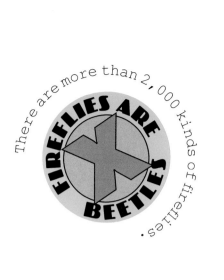

There are more than 2,000 kinds of fireflies.

FIREFLIES ARE BEETLES

Humans eat more beetles than any other insects.

Most are eaten when newly hatched.

TOP FIVE XTREME BEETLES

Xtreme Beetle #5

A Painful Bite The Devil's coach-horse beetle is the top predator in European gardens. It hides under rocks and logs. This one-inch-long (2.5 cm) beetle has extreme defenses. It can raise its rear like a scorpion. It can give off a stinky odor from its belly. This beetle bites hard with its powerful mandibles. It may appear scary, but this beetle helps gardeners by eating pests such as slugs, mites, and snails.

Some beetles can survive underwater by breathing air trapped under their wings.

Beetle Babies

Baby beetles come out of eggs. The eggs are laid by a female. Featherwing beetle mothers lay only one egg at a time. The egg is half the size of the mother's body! Cowpea seed and carpet beetles may lay more than 100 eggs in a day. Mealworm beetles can lay more than 300 eggs in their lifetime.

Beetles develop through metamorphosis. This means that they change form as they grow. When baby beetles hatch, they are called larvae. They are soft. Larvae may grow for a few days, weeks, or even years. As they grow, they shed their skin. This is called molting. Then new skin grows. Sabertooth longhorn beetle larvae can grow to more than eight inches (20.3 cm) long!

Some larvae next become pupae. They do not move or eat. It may take from a few days to several months for a pupa to become an adult beetle. Some beetles skip the pupal stage. They go straight from larva to adult.

1 to **100** eggs
in a day

Beetle eggs are laid

ladybugs

3 to **7** days

Larvae hatch

Molting larvae gro

1 month

mealworms

4
to

19
days

dung beetles

3
weeks

ladybugs

1
to

3
years

Some larvae pupate

Adult beetles reproduce

Firefly and glowworm eggs and larvae

can light up just like their parents.

Xtreme Beetle #4

Hungry, Hungry Beetles Pine bark beetles are some of the most destructive beetles in the world. They are only one-fifth of an inch (0.5 cm) long, but they can destroy whole forests. From 2013 to 2015, California got little rain. The land became dry. The trees grew weak. Pine bark beetles attacked forests. The larvae chewed the insides of the trees. They destroyed more than 10 million trees!

XTRAORDINARY LIFESTYLE

Most beetles do not live in groups. Many communicate simply by producing scents. These scents are called pheromones. Beetles can smell pheromones from far away.

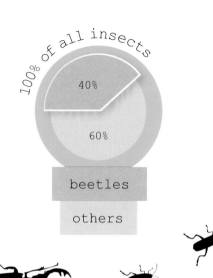

100% of all insects

40%

60%

beetles

others

BEETLE SOCIETY FACT

No other animal group has as much variety in size, color, and shape as beetles do.

A group of adult beetles is called a possi.

BEETLE POSSI

Beetle Society

Most beetles are solitary. This means that they live alone. Some beetles live in trees. Others live underground. Beetles come together to find food and create offspring. They use a variety of senses to communicate with each other.

Glowworms and fireflies are able to create light inside their bodies. This is called bioluminescence. These beetles use their lights to find mates. Different kinds of lightning bugs have unique light patterns.

Dermestid beetles use pheromones to let others know about food. These beetles eat dead animals. A group of 5,000 dermestid beetles can clean a deer skull of flesh in just a few days!

XEMPLARY SKILLS

Beetles have extreme skills that enable them to survive alone. Some beetles are talented hunters. Others are good at protecting themselves.

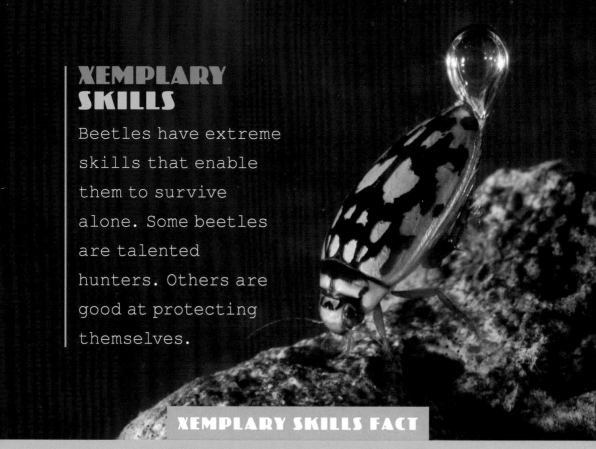

Sunburst diving beetles carry an air bubble on their rear.

This air bubble helps them breathe underwater.

Some Australian ground beetles are nearly three inches (7.6 cm) long. They hunt mice.

Caterpillar hunters can
quickly climb trees to find
a meal. Assassin beetles can inject
poison into their prey. Then the prey cannot move.
The beetles use their mouthparts like a straw to
suck out the prey's insides.

    Beetles also use extreme skills to protect
themselves. Bombardier beetles have two special
substances inside their bodies. When threatened,
the beetles will shoot the substances out of their
rear. They combine to create an explosion!

    The firefly protects itself by sending a bitter-
tasting blood through its body. Its blood is also
poisonous to some animals.

Xtreme Beetle #3

Amazon Giant The titan beetle grows up to 6.5 inches (16.5 cm) long. It is the largest beetle in South America. It is also one of the biggest insects in the world. Titan beetles are not aggressive. But they will hiss and bite to protect themselves. The beetles' mandibles are so strong that they can break a pencil! This beetle is in danger of dying out. Humans are destroying its rainforest home.

XASPERATING CONFLICT

Many beetles have adapted to live among humans. But some beetles are pests. This can cause conflicts between beetles and humans. Other beetles help the environment.

Beetle Survival

Pesky beetles may destroy trees or eat crops. Young Asian long-horned beetles live inside trees. They burrow beneath the bark. The beetles cause the trees to die within 10 to 15 years. They have destroyed more than 120,000 trees in the United States!

Another pest is the flea beetle. It is small, but it can destroy vegetable crops. Some farmers use other beetles to kill pests. Ladybugs are powerful carnivores. They eat other beetles that are pests.

Scientists use dermestid beetles to clean animal bones for museum displays.

Some beetles are in danger of dying out because of human activity. When humans use poisons to kill pests, helpful insects are also killed. This may be why the American burying beetle is endangered. These beetles help the environment. A pair of beetles finds a dead animal. The beetles bury it and lay eggs in it. The larvae hatch and feed on the animal. This cleans the forest floor.

The fly-catching rove beetle gives off an odor that attracts flies.

The beetle then captures and eats the flies.

Xtreme Beetle #2

Heavyweight Beetle Goliath beetles are enormous. In fact, they are the heaviest insects in the world. Adults can weigh 3.5 ounces (99.2 g). That is as much as a deck of playing cards. They can grow to more than 4.5 inches (11.4 cm) long. These beetles are also extremely strong. They can lift more than 850 times their own weight! They have sharp claws used for climbing. They also have long horns used for fighting.

Dung beetles are named for the animal droppings they roll into balls.

When June beetles are touched, they may make a huffing sound like heavy breathing.

Goliath beetle larvae grow underground for five months.

During spring and summer, a female ladybug can lay up to 1,000 eggs.

Dung beetle larvae eat solid dung, while their parents suck up the dung's liquid.

Mealworms, often fed to pet birds and lizards, are the larvae of darkling beetles.

Deathwatch beetles may eat furniture and wood floors in people's homes.

In the Kalahari Desert, people use poisonous leaf beetle larvae to tip their hunting arrows.

Hercules beetles use their two- to three-inch (5.1–7.6 cm) pincers to fight each other.

Scientists examining old wood found wood-boring beetle larvae still alive after 51 years!

Ladybugs produce a stinky fluid in their legs that tastes bad to predator

Leaf beetle moms stamp their feet to scare away egg-eating predators.

Convergent lady beetles travel in large swarms of up to 80,000 members in the spring!

People in Asia once

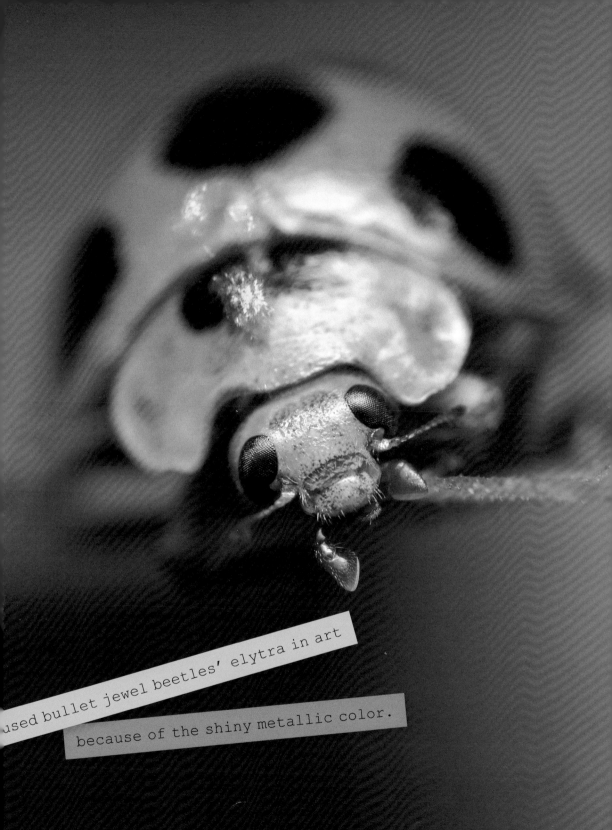

used bullet jewel beetles' elytra in art because of the shiny metallic color.

Xtreme Beetle #1

Wrestling Champions Dung beetles are the strongest animals in the world. They can push or pull more than 1,100 times their own body weight uphill. If you were as strong as a dung beetle, you could push three school buses up a hill! Dung beetles' strength helps them find mates. Males wrestle each other to get attention from females. The strongest beetle wins the wrestling match and gets to reproduce with the female.

GLOSSARY

antennae – body parts that protrude from the head and are used for sensing surroundings

compound eyes – those made up of many parts that see in many directions at once

dung – waste matter eliminated from the body of an animal

endangered – in danger of being made extinct, or dying off

RESOURCES

"Beetles." Pest World for Kids. http://www.pestworldforkids .org/pest-guide/beetles.

Bouchard, Patrice, ed. *The Book of Beetles: A Life-Size Guide to Six Hundred of Nature's Gems*. Chicago: University of Chicago Press, 2014.

Eaton, Eric R., and Kenn Kaufman. *Kaufman Field Guide to Insects of North America*. New York: Houghton Mifflin, 2007.

"Insects." National Geographic Kids. http://kids .nationalgeographic.com/animals/hubs/insects/.

INDEX

Bee mimic beetles protect themselves by pretending to be bees.